La glace

Melvin et Gilda Berger

Texte français d'Alexandra Martin-Roche

Catalogage avant publication de Bibliothèque et Archives Canada

Berger, Melvin

La glace / Melvin et Gilda Berger ; texte français d'Alexandra Martin-Roche

(Lire et découvrir)
Traduction de: Ice.
Pour les 4 à 6 ans.
ISBN 978-0-545-98167-5

1. Glace--Ouvrages pour la jeunesse. I. Berger, Gilda II. Martin-Roche, Alexandra III. Titre. IV. Collection: Lire et découvrir

QC926.37.B46814 2010   j551.31   C2009-904527-3

Photographies : Couverture : Robert Carlyle Day / PhotoResearchers Inc.; p. 1 : John Hyde / Bruce Coleman Inc.; p. 3 : Jason Lindsey / Dembinsky Photo Assoc.; p. 4 : Eunice Harris / Photo Researchers, Inc.; p. 5 : Mike Brinson / The Image Bank / Getty Images; p. 6 : Digital Vision Ltd. / SuperStock; p. 7 : Michael Newman / PhotoEdit; p. 8 : Kevin Fleming / Corbis; p. 9 : Bryan & Cherry Alexander / Photo Researchers, Inc.; p. 10 : Wedigo Ferchland / Bruce Coleman Inc.; p. 11 : Dan Guravich / Photo Researchers, Inc.; p. 12 : Michael Keller / Corbis; p. 13 : Flip Nicklin / Minden Pictures; p. 14 : Laura Riley / Bruce Coleman Inc.; p. 15 : George D. Lepp / Corbis; p. 16 : Dwight Kuhn.

Recherche de photos : Sarah Longacre

Copyright © Melvin et Gilda Berger, 2005.
Copyright © Éditions Scholastic, 2010, pour le texte français.
Tous droits réservés.

Il est interdit de reproduire, d'enregistrer ou de diffuser, en tout ou en partie, le présent ouvrage par quelque procédé que ce soit, électronique, mécanique, photographique, sonore, magnétique ou autre, sans avoir obtenu au préalable l'autorisation écrite de l'éditeur. Pour toute information concernant les droits, s'adresser à Scholastic Inc., 557 Broadway, New York, NY 10012, É.-U.

Édition publiée par les Éditions Scholastic, 604, rue King Ouest, Toronto (Ontario) M5V 1E1

5 4 3 2 1   Imprimé au Canada 120   10 11 12 13 14

Comme la glace est belle!

Tu peux patiner sur la glace.

Tu peux faire des sauts et des pirouettes.

Info-glace
La glace conserve les aliments au frais longtemps.

La glace est froide.

Elle rend les boissons froides.

Info-glace
Les gens se servent d'outils pour casser la glace.

La glace est dure.

Les Inuits construisent des maisons en glace.

Parfois, la glace est épaisse.

Info-glace
La glace du pôle Sud est trois fois plus profonde que le Grand Canyon.

Les phoques font des trous dedans.

Parfois, la glace est mince.

Les poissons nagent en dessous.

La glace flotte.

La glace fond.

La glace, c'est fascinant!

To Pam —
Find your inner hero!

GARGLE THE GOOSE

by Andrew Perry

Illustrated by Elaine Verstraete

Andrew Perry

GARGLE THE GOOSE

Copyright © 2014 by Andrew William Perry

Illustrations Copyright © 2015 by Elaine Verstraete

Graphic Design by Elaine Verstraete

Printed by CreateSpace, An Amazon.com Company

Website: www.garglegoose.com

ISBN: 978-1519500472

This book is dedicated to you, the reader of this book. Gargle and I thank you from the bottoms of our goosy hearts. I would also like to thank my wife, Kim, for loving and believing in me. Always, and in all ways.

Table of Contents

A Brief Note from Your Narrator.....................1

Chapter One: A Plan Is Hatched.....................5

Chapter Two: A Plan Gone Awry.....................10

Chapter Three: Luckless the Donkey.....................14

Chapter Four: The Farmer and the Fox.....................19

Chapter Five: Galahad the Great.....................29

Chapter Six: Coronation.....................45

Goosolalia.....................58

A Brief Note From Your Narrator

This book was written with fearless readers in mind. As a result of lengthy consultations with my wise goose advisers, we decided that it was necessary to tell this ripping adventure with some reasonably challenging language and a handful of unfamiliar terms. To be the most useful narrator for you demanded that I provide an instructive "goosololia" which introduces you to significant features of goose culture. You can refer to this before, during or after the tale, and as often or as little as you need.

Here at the beginning of our journey together, it is also necessary for me to acknowledge that reading is not always easy. Anything that you truly value rarely is. Think of words as candles in the darkness that will always be there for you, lighting your way, as you seek to express the noble goose who lives within us all. Words give expression to our hidden thoughts and allow us to share our secret selves with each other, much like we are doing at this very moment.

Words can be both your joy and your armor against a world that will constantly lay challenges along the thorny path to your inner hero. For never doubt, my legions of daring readers, that like Gargle you, too, are on a hero's journey through this daunting world. This expedition will require you to be plucky, resilient, and resolute in the face of conditions that can sometimes be harsh and cruel, particularly for its avid reading members. Just remember to be bold and courageous in the face of adversity.

So read on, brave adventurer, and turn the ancient page in the story that is you, and me, and everyone in between.

GARGLE THE GOOSE

by Andrew Perry

Illustrated by Elaine Verstraete

Chapter 1

A Plan Is Hatched

Gargle the goose was having a bad day. Being twelve (in goose years) was harder than he thought. So far it seemed like his age simply meant more chores, more homework, and girls who just seemed more goofy by the day. *Sheesh*–who needed them?

A year ago, when he was six, twelve looked so exciting and fun. When he was a downy gosling, his older brothers and sisters had seemed so big, so adventurous, so cool. Now he was the age that they were back then. And he was disgruntled.

Adding to the day's general badness, Gargle was sitting in a muddy ditch. He was watching his oldest brother, Gulliver, clacking beaks with his lady friend Guinevere. They were cooing at each other with the goopiest looks that Gargle had ever seen. It seemed like all his brother was interested in talking about anymore was how long and slender Guinevere's neck was.

"Don't we *all* have long necks, for peep's sake?" he squonked under his breath. Gargle felt his breakfast of bug mash gurgle in the back of his throat. He gulped it back down, struggling to understand how his brother could be so silly. *"Silly as a goose."* Suddenly, the old saying made a lot of sense.

It was almost impossible for Gargle to believe now, but Gulliver had been the youngest goose in the history of their gaggle to guide them in their migration. One short spring ago, when Gulliver had been only eleven-and-one-half years old, he had guided their gaggle to the goosing grounds in greater Canada. Their father, Galen, often honked about it in reverent terms. This leadership role was a high honor in the goose world and brought much praise and admiration to the Gosworth family name.

Gargle noodled his webbed toes in the mud and turned away from the spectacle of Gulliver and Guinevere. Looking over his wing, he gawked at his two best friends, Gertie and Gabbie. They were having one of their usual squabbles. Today it was over what you called more than one goose.

"Gooses," said Gertie.

"Geeses," said Gabbie.

Gargle knew that tomorrow they would switch sides without even realizing it. Yesterday's quarrel was over what to call their gaggle.

"Canada Goose," said Gabbie.

"Canadian Goose," said Gertie.

Last week it was Barnacle Goose versus Cackling Goose. These squabbles were never-ending.

Gargle gave a great, goosy honk of disgust. He had his eyes on something far grander than this endless squabble, for today was the Great Departure, when all the gaggles gathered together to go.

He gazed at the sky as thousands–*tens* of thousands–of geeses noisily arrived at the staging area. More V-shapes than he could count veered through the air. They trumpeted their excitement at seeing their far-flung families and friends.

Despite his goosedown coat, Gargle shivered from the chill in the autumnal Canadian air. Several gaggles banked in just over his head, furrowing the surface of the lake with big blooms of water formed by their triangular goosefeet. In a few short minutes the flyway would be cleared for their gaggle and the green light given for them to ascend to cruising altitude. For the last week, he had been hearing his internal compass whisper the command, "Go south," in his little, feathery ear-hole.

He did not know it yet, but Gargle was hatching a plan.

He turned to Gabbie and Gertie and honked, "What would you say if I told you I'm going to take point in our journey to the southern wintering grounds?" Gabbie

coughed out a sticky wad of chewed-up bug butts and gaped at Gargle with her pink tongue flopping out. Gertie's eyes went wider than two ostrich eggs.

"Point," as any young goose knows, is reserved for the strongest and most respected members of a gaggle. To earn this respect you have to prove yourself through brave or responsible actions, like being a distinguished teacher in Flight School, or completing a challenge like building a sturdy nest, or outsmarting a hungry fox.

Gargle had done none of these things.

He opened his beak to squabble with his friends, but before a single angry word could come out, he heard the resonating peal of a tolling bell. And then the world went white. Then red. Then black.

When the lights came back on, he found himself sprawled headlong on the ground. Somewhere far away the dull, lumpy note of a cowbell sounded tunelessly. One side of his face was completely splattered in mud. His head felt like a fumbled football.

"What happened?" he honked in a wobbly voice.

"Oh, I'm really quite terribly sorry," squonked the fattest duck Gargle had ever seen. "I haven't quite perfected my landings yet," he explained. The portly duck held out his wings, and with a colossal effort, pulled Gargle to his feet. He gallantly offered Gargle a lacy white handkerchief for the muck on his face.

"Let me introduce myself," he quacked. "My name is Delbert. Delbert the Duck."

Delbert bowed as low as his big belly would allow. "I have recently escaped from a foie gras factory."

"What's fwa gra?" Gabbie honked in a nasally voice.

"It's fattened duck or goose liver, my young fledgling," explained Delbert. "I have just spent the last six months eating corn mush through a tube."

"That doesn't sound so bad," said Gertie, her hungry curiosity awakened by their rotund new visitor.

"Yeah, where do *I* go to join?" horked Gabbie.

"I can see how it might sound like paradise," Delbert gabbled gloomily, "but it's not all it's cracked up to be."

"Wha d'you mean?" asked Gertie.

But before Delbert could get another word out, Gargle angrily broke in. "Hey! What about me?" he said in a wounded voice. "Sometime today, I'm going to take point!"

Delbert looked Gargle over from beak to toes, and wingtip to wingtip. He broke into a duckish laugh. "I hardly think so," he said bluntly.

But before Gargle could even be offended, an excited wave of honks rippled over the gaggle. "Green light!" he heard many familiar, goosy voices exclaiming. He made a fowl face at Delbert and turned to go. Without even a goodbye, Gargle, Gabbie, and Gertie took their places near the ends of their respective lines. When it was their turn, they stepped into the headwind and their gaggles took flight.

They were heading south.

Chapter 2

A Plan Gone Awry

Several days had passed since Gargle announced his intention to take point in that autumn's Great Departure. Each time the highest ranking members of his gaggle rotated in and out of the front of the wedge, Gabbie and Gertie gave him squinchy faces and sniggered gleefully behind his back. Flying at the front of the V took a tremendous amount of energy compared to those who drafted behind the goose on point. Even at the back of the line, Gargle was bone tired by the end of the first day of traveling. By the end of the second day, he felt like a dozen scrambled eggs.

He was worried. The entire federation of gaggles had already made it to the second of only three rest stop ponds along their migration route. He knew he would have to make his move tomorrow, or not at all.

On the morning of the third day, just before the sun began to rise, Gargle woke up early and shook the feathers from the attic of his weary head. He scarfed down a quick breakfast of soggy hot dog buns and guzzled an energy drink made from puddle water and lightning bugs. "Control tower to Mother Goose …" he squelched in a scratchy voice to himself to boost his dwindling courage. "It's GO time!"

Gabbie and Gertie were not in his gaggle, but because their families were so close, they always traveled together. He paused to listen to their loud snores. As geeses have done since the dawn of time, their beaks were tucked beneath their left wings. Their brassy snoring sounded like an antique Model T horn getting violently squeezed by an infuriated monkey.

Gargle gawped at the eastern horizon where the sun was just cresting the edge of the world and smiling on a new day. The bees were beezing, the birds were burbling, the butterflies were buttering, and Gargle's mood was blossoming into a black thunderhead.

"Don't be a yellow gosling," he whispered to himself. He swung his little foot in a lazy arc and connected squarely with Gabbie's sizeable rear end. The unexpected force of the kick knocked Gabbie goose-over-tea-cup directly into Gertie's lap, launching both of them into a honking tangle of squonking, feathery fury. Gargle guffawed joylessly at their distress. When they calmed down, he offered them some of his energy drink, which they gulped greedily.

"Makin' your move today?" asked Gabbie in a snarky voice. He was rubbing his sore bum that now contained the exact shape of Gargle's muddy, webbed foot. "Wait and see," Gargle answered in a determined voice. Gabbie and Gertie rolled their beady black eyes at each other.

Gertie spotted a soggy hotdog bun and ambushed it before Gabbie could make his move, inspiring another squabbling roll in the muck. "Goslings," was all Gargle could say.

An hour later the gaggles were airborne once more. Moments before the green light for final departure, Gargle had pirated his father's spare pair of gaggle goggles, which he was now wearing. They tottered precariously on the crest of his beak, too large for his small head. The advantage was that they covered most of his fluffy face, giving him the look of a higher-ranking gaggle member. This was the detail he was counting on in his hastily hatched plan.

As the miles reeled by beneath them, Gargle moved steadily up the left leg of the V. Just before lunchtime he had made it all the way to the second position, just behind point. He was flailing his wings impatiently when his golden opportunity suddenly presented itself. One of his Aunts, who had been on point for an hour, honked at the begoggled Gargle to take charge. His little goosy heart leapt up the length of his long throat.

He had just been handed the reins of the skein. He was in command!

Their cruising altitude was just below a stormy weather pattern that was creeping up the eastern coast. Gargle's first decision was to move them up through the murky cloud formation. When they emerged from the cloud bank, the sun burst in a radiant shower of warm, magnificent glows–more hues and tints and shades and washes of brilliant golden colors than Gargle ever imagined could exist.

It was glorious!

He had never felt more alive than at this exact moment. He could feel the skin beneath his feathers breaking out in a flood of goose bumps. He was tempted to break into a barrel roll but thought better of it because of the gaggle's tight formation. *Oh, what the heck,* he thought. He rotated once around the axis of his butt. It was so fun he had to do it a second time. On the third roll he realized he had strayed a little too far from his flight path. When he banked to regain it a sickening feeling dropped his stomach into his feet.

He looked to starboard. Nothing.

He looked to port. Nothing again.

Panic pounded through his brainpan like a prickly porcupine. Where was his gaggle? He searched through his plan, hoping to discover what had gone wrong, but his mind was an empty, broken egg shell. As if struck by lightning, he suddenly remembered one of the most important lessons in his flight school training. He had gone above the hard deck! The biggest rookie mistake of all. And then it dawned on him.

He was alone.

Chapter 3

Luckless the Donkey

It had been nearly a week since Gargle had tried to hijack his gaggle's point position. He was certain that he could manage a solo flight to the southern goosing grounds. But any welcome he might receive would be colder than a tin bucket of snowman pee.

He trembled as images of his family's disappointment and disapproval flapped, fluttered, and flailed through his flustered fancy. No, he could not face them. His father most of all.

Gargle's belly was gurgling. He had been spending most of his recent afternoons poking forlornly through stinky dumpsters in dark alleys behind vacant strip malls. All he had eaten for the last three days was some melted ice cream that tasted like a sausage milkshake, and half of a chewed corn dog rolled in chocolate sauce and kitty litter. Worst of all was an old, gooey brick of yellow Jello with an oddly shaped grape which, when he bit into it, turned out to be a dog turd.

He had washed down these repulsive meals with some warm grape soda from a dented can that he carried on a dirty string around his neck. On the mouth of the can was a lady's large, red lipstick smudge. Inside was a dead bee.

In one unfortunate incident he had desperately attempted to pilfer an unguarded bag of french fries from a round man with a very hairy back. It had not gone well. He longed for a chubby, pink nightcrawler or a large, juicy grasshopper.

Gargle was spending a lot of time wallowing in the muddy puddle of his own misery. He had taken to muttering to himself, a common habit of solitary wanderers. And worse yet, he was not only constantly hungry and lonely and hungry. He knew that being alone was a very dangerous situation for a young goose to be in.

He had to find help.

On the Sunday morning of the seventh day of his exile, Gargle decided that town living no longer suited him. It was time to skeedaddle to the country. Fat, red apples and cool, clear ponds were calling to him.

That afternoon, Gargle found himself waddling down the dry, gravelly shoulder of a narrow country lane. He had decided that his flying days were over. He was no longer worthy of his wings. His father's spare pair of gaggle goggles bounced uselessly around the base of his neck like a ring too big for a finger. He sighed for the eleventeenth time that day when suddenly a distressed braying shattered the stillness of the quiet autumn air. It was the saddest sound Gargle had ever heard.

Overcome by curiosity, he ran as quickly as his little feet could carry him over a short hill and under a long row of scarlet hedges. In the middle of a small dirt path was the most curious sight. For it was there, suspended by his harness, that Gargle beheld a luckless donkey dangling in midair. A heavy cart, resting on its tailgate, was clearly too much for the feeble donkey's meager proportions.

He turned to look at Gargle with his big, sad donkey eyes and a single tear ran down his nose. Dark, wet trails in his snout fur led to runny nostrils. It was apparent that the donkey had been engaging in a lengthy spell of crying.

"Are you stuck?" asked Gargle, suddenly realizing with an embarrassed shock just how ridiculous this question was.

The donkey gave him a stinging look. "No, this is a game we donkeys play when we're bored," answered Luckless with an icy note of sarcasm.

"Have you been crying?" asked Gargle. This question was worse than the first, causing the gloomy donkey to break into a new round of sobbing. Gargle stepped forward sheepishly to pull at the clasp on the harness buckle with his beak. Luckless began to kick his hooves like he was riding a bicycle, but there was only empty air beneath him. With a mighty hee haw, he crashed in a bony heap at Gargle's feet and let out an airy snort, followed by an enormous and musical fart.

"That was poorly done," said Luckless.

"What was I supposed to do?" answered Gargle. "Lower you gently to the ground and give you a big, wet kiss?"

"That sounds better than what I got!" replied Luckless, who slowly hauled himself to his feet with a gripe and a groan.

Gargle looked him up and down. The coarse fur on the donkey's back was a glum, gloomy gray, his head a mottled, mothy moccasin, his rump a blotchy, blemished brown. He looked like he had been sewn together with patches from the backside of an old hobo's britches.

"What are you doing here?" asked Luckless. "Why aren't you flying south with the rest of your herd?" His voice was raspy like a gruff, croaky bullfrog's.

"It's a *gaggle*," replied Gargle. "And I have released myself on my own recognizance."

"What does that mean?" asked Luckless. A confused look passed over his long face like a brisk ripple of wind over the surface of a winter pond.

"It means that I'm a free agent. My own man A goose about town."

Luckless's teary eyes crossed with miscomprehension.

Gargle pulled on his gaggle goggles. "I'm an independent goose now. I've decided to pursue a liberated life of exploits, explorations, adventures, voyages, journeys, and quests," he said with a jubilant look on his face.

"When do you lift off?" asked Luckless.

"Today!" said Gargle in his firmest tone. "But I don't fly anymore. I'll be walking instead," he said, his voice deflating like the flatulent flapping of an emptying balloon. Gargle pinched his face into a look that clearly said he did not want to talk about the reasons why.

"Sounds tiring," replied the donkey in his froggy voice. "Would you like a companion who can carry you on his back?"

Gargle had not considered how much waddling would be required to undertake his adventures. NO! he wanted to say. But in his imagination he saw the lonely, hungry miles and weary years unspooling beneath his blistered, webby feet.

"Why not?" he replied.

Without further ado, the spindly donkey lunged clumsily forward and roughly lifted the startled young goose onto his bumpy back. It felt like a dusty burlap sack filled with broken ballpeen hammers, but it beat walking.

"Onward to the future!" holler-honked Gargle.

Chapter 4

The Farmer and the Fox

Time turned like a rusty wheel.

Days turned steadily to weeks, and weeks gradually to months. The brilliant colors of fall surrendered to the solemn darkness of winter. The goose and the donkey spent Christmas behind a rundown gas station next to an old, neglected interstate.

As his gift to Luckless, Gargle shared the story of how he had come into his present circumstances. Luckless listened closely, shaking his narrow head at certain points in the tale. At other points he broke into tears. Luckless admitted with shame that he had nothing but friendship to offer Gargle.

It was more than enough.

As any vagabond can tell you, meals are hard to come by when you're on the road without a nickel to your name and no experience of the wide, wide world. Nearly every trashcan, ashcan, wastebin, dustbin, and dumpster for miles around was guarded by bullying beasts who relied on the squawks of their noisy seagull informers. On their journey, the two travelers had experienced terrifying run-ins with three angry, speeding motorists; two sleepy but very grouchy rattlesnakes; and one cranky and confrontational black bear. And the less said about the gangs of spraypaint-wielding teens, the better.

But all things considered, the two fared well. One cold and fusty winter afternoon, Gargle and Luckless were wending their way along a twisty forest path when they heard the distant munch of crunching feet in frosted leaves. As they listened, the sound of tuneless human whistling reached their ears. The melody resembled a troubling jumble of the tear-jerking ditty "How Can I Miss You If You Won't Go Away?" and the heart-rending ballad "The Last Word In Lonesome Is Me." But mostly it just sounded like a gassy duck kicking an accordion.

Hard experience had taught them the powerful lesson that it was best to yield the trail at the approach of a stranger. The waddly goose and the clumsy donkey bustled off the path to hide behind an enormous Southern Oak tree. Before long, an old, grizzled farmer came strolling into view. His shirt was grubby, his front teeth were missing, he needed a shave, his pants were droopy, his shoes were covered with manure, and the sour look on his baggy face marked him as not the friendliest of characters. A soiled baseball cap was perched atop his dented head. Above the torn bill it announced, "Be-Hind BBQ: Best Roasted Goose in the South!"

Before Gargle could stop himself, a muffled yelp snarfed from his beak. At the sound, the farmer's knobby head shot in their direction. A suspicious expression was written all over his gnarled mug.

"You there!" he croaked. "This here's private property!!" He produced a pointy-looking weapon from the deep pocket on his hip. "I'm gonna gitcha," he snarled as he sprung toward them.

Fear surged like a dog bite through the traveling companions. In the twinkle of a gosling feather, they found themselves plunging headlong through the gloomy woods to escape the old man's wrath. Cruel branches reached out to apply painful red stripes across their faces and backs. In no time at all, Gargle was limp with exhaustion, and he paused to catch his ragged breath. To his dismay, he discovered that Luckless had vanished.

His little heart turned over like a flapjack and proceeded to hammer more fiercely against the inside of his chest. At that moment, a dreadful hee hawing sawed through the barren trees. Swallowing his rising panic, Gargle doubled back to find his friend. He followed the frightened braying to the lip of an abandoned well. When he peered over the crumbling rim, he spied poor Luckless seated on his bony rear at the bottom of the stony pit.

"Help?" was all Luckless could squeak.

"Hold your horses ... I mean donkeys!" ordered Gargle. "We've got to find a way to get you free before the farmer finds us!"

Luckless gulped down a sob.

"Wait here ... I'll be right back," said Gargle.

Luckless's long, floppy ears flattened in disgust. "Fine, but I was about to get some black coffee and a jelly donut," he replied.

"What? Why??" said Gargle in a shocked voice.

"Oh yeah, *squonk squonk*," he cackled nervously. Down in that hole, he realized, Luckless was not going anywhere. Gargle spun on his heel and waddled back into the confusion of the scary woods.

An hour passed. Then two. Gargle was getting desperate. He had to find someone, *anyone*, who could help him. He sat down on a rotten stump and gave in to a hard, heavy, honking cry. When he was done, he blew his beak on a dead leaf.

Just then, a soft, velvety voice breathed into his ear-hole. "Why are you crying, little goose?"

Startled, Gargle found himself staring into the crescent-shaped eyes of a fabulously fetching fox. Before he could gather his wits, he blurted in a blubbery voice, "My donkey friend is stuck down an old well, and I don't know how to get him out."

"Come with me to my cozy den," she crooned in a silky growl. "I can help you solve your predicament."

"I don't know …" stammered the bamboozled goose.

"Yes," exclaimed the fox, "I have hot broth, a warm hearth, and a snug bed in my spare chamber. We can get you out of your pickle in the morning."

Gargle felt powerless before the spellbinding glow of the fox's cinnamon-colored glare.

"I'm your friend," she said.

He followed her into her warm burrow down under the earth. But before he could go more than three waddling steps, Gargle felt the flat, clanging note of a gong ping-ponging around the inside of his head. This strange sensation was attended by a brilliant, shimmery light. As he peered at it, the illumination faded to a tiny white dot before it crackled to black with an electric snap.

When he awoke, he was not sure how long he had been away. Peculiar, doodly shapes swam through his vision. He also noticed that he could not move his wings or legs. He shook his head and the noodly forms took on slightly more focus.

On the kitchen table lay a cast-iron frying pan with the distinct shape of his head walloped into the underside. "That's odd," a distracted, dreamy voice mused in his muddled imagination. The pleasant smell of cooked turnips and onions wafted to his nostrils, while cheery flames crackled and licked up the sides of a blackened stew pot.

"How nice," he thought with a sense of gratitude. "It must be suppertime."

A rougher voice in his head rudely pushed the first one aside and shouted,

"WAKE UP, YOU GOOFY GOOSE! *YOU'RE* WHAT'S FOR SUPPER!"

"Oh no!" he said out loud. "I'm going into the kettle!"

"Awake are we?" barked the fox, as she carved another carrot into the pot.

Despite the feathers in his head, Gargle knew he had to think fleetly on his feetly. "I have a friend …" he began hesitantly.

"A donkey, isn't it?" the fox asked pleasantly.

"Yes, a very smart, very strong, very brave donkey who has a very classified secret," he bluffed.

"Hmmm, …" hummed the fox, looking up from her carrot with mild interest. "And what might this *very classified secret* be?"

Multiple fibs stampeded around Gargle's foggy brain like an angry bull through a dandelion patch. "His … owner…" he stuttered. "Yes … this donkey's owner has a huge ring of keys that he always wears on his belt."

"What of it?" asked the fox, noticeably losing interest.

"The largest key is to a colossal hen house!" he exclaimed. "With more hens than you could stew in a lifetime!"

The carrot thudded to the floor. "I wouldn't be too sure of that," she said, a note of excitement creeping into her honeyed voice.

"But he's one mean, nasty, cruel, malicious, unpleasant donkey," said Gargle, warming to his subject. "He's also one stingy, miserly, tightfisted, parsimonious, penny-pinching donkey too," he added for good measure.

Delicious images began frolicking wildly through the fox's imagination. Chicken soup, chicken stew, chicken pie, broiled chicken, boiled chicken, seared chicken, speared chicken, roasted chicken, toasted chicken.

Her mouth began to water. Her tongue lolled out of the side of her mouth.

"You'd have to do something awfully generous for him to give up the location of where his owner lives," suggested Gargle.

"I could dig him out of that well!" offered the fox. "Would that do the trick?" She examined him with bright, greedy eyes.

"I believe it would," he answered.

The fox began moving toward the door.

"Where are you going?" demanded Gargle in alarm.

"To free your donkey friend," she answered snippily, as if it were the most obvious answer in the world.

"But you'll need *me*," he argued. "Otherwise the old coot won't know who you are. Then you're likely to get nothing but a swift kick for your troubles."

"That's wise advice," she agreed.

Her face turned sinister. "No running off, though," she threatened darkly. She untied his bonds, adding, "I can run much faster than you."

They hastily left the den, leaving the stew pot bubbling madly over the fire. When they reached the lip of the ancient well, Gargle's shadow fell like a dark phantom across Luckless's wretched face.

"You sure took your sweet time," he said to the goose's outline looming over him. "I thought you were never coming back," he sniffed. When he raised a hoof to shade his eyes, Luckless noticed that Gargle was not alone.

"This is our new companion, Friendly Fox," said Gargle, reluctantly introducing her. "She's going to dig you out of that well for the price of a secret," he said in a strangled voice.

"And what might that secret be?" asked Luckless.

"You're going to tell her how to get the key ring from your owner, right?" said Gargle, winking his long lashes and stamping his little foot in the dust.

"Huh?" said Luckless stupidly.

"Your owner? The key ring?" Gargle suggested in exasperation, trying unsuccessfully to give Luckless a meaningful look.

"I don't *have* an owner anymmmOUCH ..." Before he could finish his thought, a sturdy stone struck him right between the eyes. In the dirt at Gargle's feet was a mysterious hollow precisely the size of the stone. He stood with an innocent look on his face and grime on his foot.

"Right. Yes," Luckless hemmed and hawed. "The key ring. It's yours," he promised the fox. The fox was an expert digger. Before long she had Luckless out of his prison no worse for wear. Luckless did a happy little donkey dance at being out of the well. "My thanks, m'lady," he told the fox.

"Save it," she snapped at him. "Where's this owner of yours?"

"This way," said Luckless. He threw a look of utter bewilderment at Gargle and they set off through the cheerless trees.

Gargle and Luckless trudged through the woods with despondent looks on their faces, the fox following closely behind. What were they to do? What new and terrible experience was next? It seemed their situation just kept getting worse and worse. They wandered for a mile. Then another.

"Where is he?" the fox kept insisting. "If you're hoodwinking me, it's into the kettle with both of you!"

At the third mile, just as they were about to give up, a ramshackle barn roof peeked through the canopy of the dead branches overhead. "There it is," Luckless announced uncertainly.

The fox shoved her way between the two companions and stepped out of the edge of the woods into a dry, lifeless meadow. The tumbledown barn seemed to be sinking into itself. Two empty windows hung on either side of a large sliding door. Their crooked jambs were wrathful eyes standing in judgment of the building's infrequent visitors. A shiny, new padlock hung from the door clasp.

The fox slinked slyly across the field to squint through a lopsided hole in the wall. When she peered in, her crafty eyes grew bigger than two goose eggs. She motioned them over to eyeball the situation for themselves. Gargle peeked through a gap between the old, weather-beaten boards. To his horror, he found himself staring at the back of the grizzled farmer who had run them off earlier in the day. But even more dreadfully, the farmer was sticking a long tube down a goose's throat, force feeding him his supper. The poor goose looked swollen and miserable. But when Gargle looked closer, his heart dropped to the bottom of his feet.

As far as he could see, row upon grimy row of hundreds–*no thousands*–of geeses were lying in dirty puddles of their own filth. He blinked his eyes, certain that they were lying to him. But there was no denying the awful truth.

This was his federation of gaggles.

Chapter 5

Galahad the Great

As the pallid sun began its late winter slant toward the rim of the western horizon, Gargle's dark face was filled with uncertainty. A day, and a night, and most of another day had passed since their ghastly discovery. Gargle was finding it difficult to push the troubling images out of his mind.

The previous night he had dreamed that the farmer's gnarled hands were closing around his long neck. When Gargle had looked into the farmer's warped face, he had seen his own, black with anger, his dark eyes the color of muddy puddles through which a furious child had recently stomped. Gargle had awoken with a strangled honk, bathed in the gravy of his own sweat. A pale crescent moon skated through the peaceful night sky, just beyond the reach of the tallest trees. The dark fingers of their branches beckoned the thin sliver of light into their tightfisted grasp.

Gargle lay still as a stone, listening to the raggedy rhythm of Luckless's robust snores. What were they going to do? The question whispered itself into his earhole again and again, tormenting him with his inability to reach an answer. Over the last day and a half, while Gargle and Luckless had been hopelessly spinning their wheels, the fox had exhibited a frantic picture of industriousness. She spied on the farmer day and night, learning his habits and patterns. She peppered the duo with endless questions:

"What time did he get out of bed? What did he eat for breakfast? Did he own a car? A truck? A tractor? A bicycle? Was he married? Did he have any business partners? Who did he call on the telly-o-phone? Why didn't he ever bathe? Was that the only shirt he owned? How old was he? What was that smell? Could someone actually survive on nothing but boloney sandwiches and red soda? What radio shows did he listen to in the evenings? What time did he go to bed? How long did he sleep? What was he endlessly mumbling? muttering? murmuring? stammering? yammering?"

And the quivering question that quavered above all the rest: "Where did he keep

his ring of keys?"

The fox's limited patience with Gargle and Luckless was stretching awfully thin. Sick of seeing them sitting on their lumpy backsides, she had ordered them to lurk outside the farmer's kitchen window after moonrise, where they currently found themselves.

"What are we going to do?" whispered Gargle for the eleventh time.

They were skulking on either side of a crooked window that faced the overgrown backyard. A bare bulb drooped over the filthy sink, throwing panes of dirty light on the cold ground between them.

"Shush," answered Luckless in as loud a voice as he dared, "he'll hear you." The window sash was open several inches, wafting the foul odor of rotting boloney to their noses.

"How long do we have to stand here?" Gargle grumbled glumly.

"Until something happens," said Luckless.

"But what if nothing does?" responded Gargle.

"Then nothing," said Luckless, getting irritated.

They waited an hour. Then two. By the third hour, it appeared that nothing was going to happen. The sickle moon had made its long transit across the deep reaches of the star-flung sky. Just as they were readying to leave, a heart-rending jangle pierced the night, causing the duo to nearly expire with fright. They flattened themselves against the clapboard wall.

The drowsy farmer entered the kitchen to answer the phone. He appeared to be quite cross. "Hello?" he snarled into the heavy, black receiver, covering it in a fine spray of spittle. They heard a gruff, muffled voice respond. It barked harsh noises into the farmer's large, misshapen ear. When Gargle opened his beak to speak, Luckless gave him an unmistakable look that said, "Zip it, goose!"

"Yes," growled the farmer to the anonymous voice at the other end of the line. "Yes … No … No … Yes … Tomorrow." Hearing only one side of the conversation made it difficult to follow.

"Huh? … Canada Geese! … Because they're everywhere!" There was a long pause while the caller droned in a flat, rambly tone. "BECAUSE THEY'RE FREE!!" the farmer finally thundered into the phone. "Yes … Foie gras … Because we'll get rich quick!"

The farmer slammed the receiver down into the cradle so hard that Gargle thought the entire phone was going to rip from the water-stained wall. The farmer stalked off in disgust. After a few moments they heard the groan of creaky springs as he returned to his bed.

"That answers a lot of questions," Luckless gently brayed to Gargle. "C'mon, let's get back to the fox."

"Oh, are we on her team now?" Gargle asked sarcastically.

Luckless made a squinchy donkey face at him. "I might have an idea," was all he said, and they reluctantly began the slow trudge back.

The fox was pleased to see the pair of misadventurers when they returned to the makeshift command center just inside the edge of the woods. "What did you find out?" she questioned them. Her voice was so sweet it seemed capable of rotting hen's teeth.

"The old man wears the keys around his neck," answered Luckless. Gargle wrinkled his brow in bewilderment. *Is that really what we found out?* he wondered silently in his feathery head. He could not recall if there were keys around the farmer's neck or not. Based on the phone call, the fact that something important was happening later that day seemed like a much more significant detail to him. Not to mention that this was a *foie gras* farm!

"How do we know he wears the keys around his neck?" blurted Gargle.

Luckless shot him a withering look. "Because we saw them as plain as the beak on your simple face." Covertly, Luckless began applying pressure on Gargle's foot with his heavy black hoof. Gargle's face turned a deep shade of scarlet and beads of sweat popped out on his ruffled noggin. The crunching pain robbed him of the ability to speak. When Luckless lifted his hoof, Gargle exhaled like an old man collapsing into a soft chair.

"What did you do that for?" he demanded.

"I thought I saw a spider," fibbed Luckless, "but it was just a dimwitted fly, so I squashed him. Now he can't buzz anymore." Gargle pondered the riddle for a moment while rubbing the webbing on his sore toe with the tip of his wing. He dimly recalled kicking the stone into Luckless's face when the donkey was down in the well. An antique lightbulb flickered to life somewhere in the goose's clammy head.

"Yes … *m'hmm* … Around his neck … *Yessiree*," sputtered Gargle to the fox. The fox's shrewd gaze raked suspiciously up one side of Gargle and down the other. She repeated it on Luckless, but if she had any doubts, she kept them to herself.

"You two had better get some sleep." It was more an order than a request. "I have a nasty surprise to prepare for our friend. An hour before sunrise, we attack," she added ominously.

She padded silently into the woods, leaving Gargle and Luckless awash in a stormy sea of doubt.

Sleep never came.

Gargle tossed and turned for an hour before finally giving up. He rolled onto his side to gaze at the donkey's saggy face. Sensing he was being watched, Luckless slowly opened a bloodshot eye to find Gargle staring at him intently.

"*What?*" said Luckless in a hoarse voice.

"Why did you tell the fox that the farmer was wearing the keys around his neck?"

After a long pause he responded, "Because that's the only information she needs from us." Gargle gave him a blank look.

"Think about it," said Luckless. "Once she has those keys, what further use are we to her? She's swift, she's strong, she's stealthy, she's smart, and she's a skilled digger …

Are we any of those things?"

"No," said Gargle sullenly.

"So we have to bluff with the only card we have," explained Luckless.

"I guess you're right," answered Gargle gloomily.

"Try to get some rest," advised Luckless. "We're going to need it later today when the feathers start to fly." Gargle shuddered, then rolled back over to continue not sleeping.

The fox returned an hour and ten minutes before dawn. She greeted the dozing pair with healthy kicks to roust them from their bedding of sticks and stones and prickly pinecones. She pointed to an old shovel sticking from the dirt.

"What do you want us to do with that?" asked Gargle while he rubbed his bleary, red eyes.

"Not *us. You*," answered the fox. "You're going to dig a hole. We'll need one later today." Gargle felt a bristly chill run up his spine, like a squirrel up a wire. "Gulp," was all he could manage to get out.

At the stroke of the hour, Luckless and the fox began creeping toward the farmer's broken-down house. The fox left Gargle with clear orders to dig a deep, rectangular hole. A "fox hole" she had called it, though he had no notion why. He could feel the merciless jaws of an imaginary trap coiling to spring with an unforgiving snap. He fervently hoped it was not *him* who it chose to bite. Gargle shook the image from his goosy head. He threw the shovel to the ground. Digging a hole was going to have to wait.

He crept behind a large, shadowy oak tree and spied the fox stealing through the gap in the kitchen window from atop Luckless's back. It was the donkey's job to stand watch. Gargle sensed that this was his moment of truth, but his icy feet felt frozen to the ground. Thinking was not going to get him out of this mess. This situation called for *action*.

Before he could question his resolve, he slipped across the yard to the darkened mouth of the yawning barn. A leathery bat plunged from the barn's broken cupola and swooped past his head. He heard a large insect yelp in distress. The giant padlock hung from a chain on the doors. It gleamed with nasty malice in the wispy rays of the rising sun. Gargle instinctively grasped that this was not the way in.

He rounded the murky corner of the barn and peered anxiously between two of the mismatched slats. To his astonishment, Delbert the Duck was snoring heavily atop a pile of soggy hay. His prodigious belly was larger than any Gargle had ever seen on a duck. Between snores, it rose and fell like a massive ship on a storm-tossed sea. Spreading around Delbert in the gloom, Gargle could just make out the inky forms of what he assumed were geeses. But because the indistinct shapes seemed so bloated, he could not be certain.

Acting on instinct, Gargle clutched a long, broken stick lying at his feet and poked it though the opening in the wall. He jabbed Delbert in his colossal rear end, which rolled like heavy waves onto a beach. Delbert's snores barely skipped a beat.

Gargle prodded him a second time. Nothing. On the third desperate try, he swung the rotten branch harder, hoping to tap Delbert on the shoulder. Instead, the branch broke in half, mid-swing. For one brief, silent moment, Gargle watched it twirl frantically through the air. But in a flash, the moment was gone. It cracked Delbert over the head so hard it knocked him clean off his perch and onto the backs of the sleeping geeses below him.

It was at that moment–the goose poets and bards would later sing–that pandemonium erupted like a congregation of enraged bees at a Sunday school picnic. Everything seemed to happen at once. Under his massive weight, the geeses that Delbert had landed on squonked like they had been shot out of a cannon. This, in turn, caused the geeses near them to sound the alarm, causing those around them to do the same. The effect was like the concussion from a bomb, rippling in percussive rollers outward from the center. In no time at all, every goose in the barn was screeching.

Gargle was finding it hard to form the slightest thought as the cacophony strained his ear-holes with the overwhelming hubbub. He stuck his head into the opening between the barn slats and shouted for his family. No one paid him the least bit of attention.

In the mayhem, one of the geeses had managed to topple a small lantern into a dry hay bale, instantaneously igniting it. The situation was hastily getting out of hand. In the blink of a bloodshot eye, it had gone from desperate, to dangerous, to downright deadly.

In a panic, Gargle pushed his weight against the wooden slats which grouchily gave way, spilling him into Delbert's ample lap. When he sat up, the slats remained stuck around his neck, framing his head like a cheery family snapshot. With a mighty leap, Gargle landed atop the tail gate of a broken-down, antique wagon, the highest point in the room.

The fire had now spread from the back of the barn to the eastern wall, and it was beginning to lick hungrily at the underside of the hay loft. There was not much time.

Geeses were howling as they scrambled in every direction, their eyes goggling with fear. Loose, oily feathers were feeding the flames, prompting the fire to dance with malevolent joy. Gargle raised his wings to his beak to shout for his family again, but before he could shape a single note, a dreadful cracking noise shattered the air as if the world itself had split down the center.

Then everything went black.

Meanwhile, back in the house, the farmer woke with a shock at what sounded like the bedlam of a clown reunion. When he opened his groggy eyes he found himself nose to snout with a frantic fox who was clawing at his neck and chest, desperately searching for something that was not there. With a mighty exertion and an unrepeatable oath, he furiously flung the fox in a furry flurry against the wall, where she sank slowly to the floor.

The farmer swung his bare feet toward the malodorous slippers he believed were resting at the foot of his bed. Unfortunately, this was the exact location where the fox had landed in a heap. Instead of his stinking slippers, the farmer's feet found the tripwire of a snare that the clever fox had ingeniously installed over a ceiling beam earlier that night. With a heave and a ho, the farmer and the fox were hoisted into the air by foot and tail in a snarling tangle of fists and fangs and foul expressions.

Witnessing this chaotic scene from outside the bedroom window, Luckless clopped rapidly toward the eruption of howls, yowls, screeches, crashes, and splashes coming from the barn. Nothing was making any sense. *Why did the fox get caught in her own trap?* he thought frantically to himself. "What should I do?" he hee-hawed in perplexed agony. He could see an angry glow coming from between the mismatched slats of the barn.

Fire!

Luckless galloped with all of his strength to the door of the barn, framed in every leaping shade of orange. The stubborn padlock frowned at him wrathfully, daring him to break it open. Luckless took it in his yellow teeth and clamped down hard, but all he managed to do was crack a bicuspid. This was no time for subtlety.

Squaring his rump to the door, he gave it a kick that could have leveled a house. The wooden timbers began to groan. He gave it another kick, this one bigger than the first. Boards splintered and fragments cut through the air like angry hornets. With one final, monumental dropkick, Luckless tore the barn door off its hinges which screamed in rusty protest. Unfortunately, the pigheaded padlock had pierced the soft underside of his rear hoof before pinwheeling into the weeds, lost forever.

With the door flung open, Luckless stared into the teeth of an oncoming goose stampede. They boiled around him in utter chaos.

"Wait! Slow down!" hollered Luckless. "Can someone help me find Gargle?"

But no one remained to listen. Too heavy from their forced feedings to take flight, every goose in the barn was hysterically waddling away, leaving Luckless standing alone in a swirling cloud of hot dust. Luckless desperately burst into the burning barn.

"Gargle! ... *Gargle!*" he shouted. The flames had now taken over the entire eastern wall and had proceeded to ignite the desiccated hay in the loft. The barn was making low, frightening moans as its heavy beams sagged beneath the fury of the ever-growing flames. Smoke and soot filled Luckless's eyes, and he began to cough heavily. He crashed into the back of an old wagon and his weight knocked a rear wheel off its rotted axle, dumping the contents of the wagon's bed onto the scuffed plank floor.

By some strange sorcery, a heavy burlap feed sack sat up and began a frantic dance, struggling like two badgers fighting over a donut. Despite the dire situation, Luckless found himself genuinely flabbergasted. Of all the things in the world he had expected to encounter in a burning barn, this was certainly not one of them.

He grasped the top of the sack in his yellow teeth and yanked with all of his might. Gargle slid from a rend in the sack. The feathers on his head were ruffled and singed, like a crooked crown on a conquered king.

"How did you get in there?" Luckless shouted over the crackle and hiss of the angry fire.

"I'm not sure," Gargle bellowed. "I heard a terrible crack and felt a huge pile of soggy somethings fall on me," he sobbed. "The next thing I knew, it was completely dark and I was hopelessly stuck in this sack. I thought my goose was cooked!" Gargle kicked away the sack in disgust.

"C'mon," roared the goose, "We have to get out of here now!"

As they turned to leave, a tiny, terrified bray came from the back corner of the barn. Luckless limped to a dead stop. Gargle crashed directly into Luckless's bony back side, knocking the goose off his feet.

"What're you doing??" screeched Gargle.

"I thought I heard something!" replied Luckless. He turned to go back.

"Oh no you don't," shouted Gargle who grabbed Luckless by the scruff of his matted mane and began manhandling him toward the door. "We're leaving! … Now!"

"But someone's still in here!" he cried, twisting free of Gargle's feathery grip. Before Gargle could make another lunge at him, Luckless plunged forward, hobbling heedlessly back toward the noise.

Gargle turned and peered out the barn door only a few feet away. Outside, a cool, sunny morning was gently unfolding. He looked in the opposite direction where Luckless had disappeared into the smoke and flames. For one brief moment, he felt his little feet carrying him toward the sweet morning sunshine. *I could just go*, he thought. *Join my family and simply fly away.* The enchanting image called to him like a mother's kiss. He looked longingly out the door once more and stepped uncertainly into the warm rays of the sun. He turned to gaze toward the back of the barn where the flames were raging like a Puritan sermon.

"Fiddlesticks fart!" he cursed under his breath as he lurched away from the tranquil morning light toward the fiery maelstrom inside. The barn was quickly becoming an inferno. The heat was so intense that, for a moment, Gargle thought it might boil him into a stew right where he stood. *Wouldn't that be peculiar*, he thought, picturing the fox's delight.

Gargle fumbled his way in the direction he had seen Luckless stumble only moments before. The visibility was dreadful. He put a wing over his face to keep the cinders out of his eyes. Over the thundering growl of the snarling fire, he could just make out the sounds of Luckless's panicky hee-haws. He pushed forward, tripping suddenly over a lumpy mass on the floor. When he picked it up, it turned out to be the feed sack. Not stopping to think, he pulled the sack over himself like a moldy coat and pushed his head through the ragged hole that Luckless had made with his teeth.

"Find them!" ordered a stern and goosy voice in his head. "You must not fail," the unyielding voice thundered. Gargle set his little jaw and marched three steps forward.

"I am with you, Gargle" encouraged the deep and steely voice. "You are not alone."

Gargle felt a jolt of strength surge through him like a live wire. He lowered his head and crept toward the struggling sound of Luckless's frantic voice. Through the thick smoke, a gray, unfocused shape resolved itself into the form of a donkey. He had found him! But what was Luckless doing?

For reasons Gargle was unable to gather, Luckless was yanking on the end of an antique rope, the other end of which disappeared into deep and frightening shadows behind a burning barn beam. Without hesitating, Gargle grabbed the rope and began tugging on it with all of his newfound strength.

For once, luck was on their side. The rope was even more rotten than the feed sack. With three savage tugs they managed to snap the rope in two. What emerged from behind the burning beam could not have surprised Gargle any more than if he had awoken that morning to discover that he was now able to lay golden eggs.

From the fiendish shadows staggered a jenny donkey, smudged from snout to rump in soot and cinders. "Thank you," she coughed gratefully, "but we don't have much time!"

In the throbbing of a single heartbeat, the blackened beams under the hay loft gave way with a hateful cry. The path out of the burning barn was now hopelessly blocked. With a look of utter defeat, Luckless nuzzled Gargle's cheek with his own. Luckless stood on three wobbly hooves as fat tears cascaded through the grime on his filthy face.

"You are my friend," he said to Gargle.

Luckless motioned to the jenny who joined them, pressing her muzzle against Gargle's neck, then gently touching it to Luckless's notched ears. "Before this ends," she said, "I'd like to know my brave rescuers' names."

Luckless bowed in a low, graceful arc. "I am Luckless the Donkey," he replied. "And this is my friend and brother, Gargle the Goose." Gargle also bowed gallantly before the jenny.

"And what is *your* name?" asked Luckless. Another beam collapsed loudly right next to them.

She looked deeply into Luckless's eyes. "My name is Loveless," she answered simply. "Loveless the Donkey."

That did it. Gargle felt an immeasurable weight lift from his shoulders. He let the filthy feed sack drop slowly to the floor. He spread his immense wings out to their full span and said, "Take me."

The two donkeys looked at him, their faces like two interlocking pieces to the same unfinished puzzle. "What?" they said together.

"Take me," he repeated. "Each of you take a wing. Pick me up and charge through that wall," he said. He pointed with his beak to the last remaining part of the room not engulfed in flames.

"I won't do it!" replied Luckless.

"You will … You must … It's all we have left," said Gargle calmly.

Another fiery beam crashed to the floor between them. Gargle stepped over the burning timber with his wings still outspread, the flames dancing in his wet eyes. He grinned at both of them.

"When you speak of me, call me Galahad."

Chapter 6

Coronation

Wind danced lightly over the surface of trembling water. The sun's smiling face shimmered in a laughing frolic of soft, sparkling silver and the gleam of glistening gold. A bare hill sloped in a gentle green tumble to caress the edge of an old mill pond. The earthy smell of spring hung heavily in the warming air.

It was here that Gargle's entire federation of gaggles had gathered beside the despondent majesty of a weeping willow, like a sleeping pillow for the head of a broken king. Its long, slender branches bent low to softly brush the water, stirring leaping ribbons of light across the pond's rippled surface. Prettily dressed in multiple nests of mockingbird finery, the willow sang its ancient song of renewal for the grave gathering of geeses.

Normally, a meeting of the federation was a loud and brassy business, as families, friends, and neighbors separated into their various gaggles to chitchat and chinwag, to chatter and natter and gossip and gabble about the goings-on in their humble, goosy lives.

But today was different. A respectful hush had descended over the usual buzz. The funeral of an exalted gander was a solemn affair.

For the last three days their gossip had focused unceasingly on only two topics. One was the spectacular scene caused by the massive barn fire. Local fire departments from all the surrounding towns had arrived in blustery knells of ear-piercing yells. The lurching swells of clanging bells and military personnel had recoiled at the sight and smell of the rising plumes and smoke that fell into the topmost rafters of the sky.

Despite hours of heroic efforts by the fire fighters, the barn had inevitably collapsed into itself like an old hound flopping onto a creaky porch. When the police searched the house they found the farmer and the fox strung upside-down from a ceiling beam, their faces redder than two bloated ticks about to pop. The illegal *foie gras* operation was quickly discovered, and the farmer was unceremoniously carted off to jail. No one knew what happened to the fox.

The second and more serious topic of gossip focused on the mysterious voice heard during the federation's escape from the burning barn. There was an outcry for information. An emergency meeting was called. Feathers flew as factions were formed between the doubters and the believers.

Finally, Gilgamesh, the federation's wise and wrinkly goose historian was called upon. After lengthy consultations with the goose bards, poets, wordsmiths, versifiers, musicians, troubadours, wandering minstrels, as well as uncountable dusty books that had to be flown in from the north at great expense, it was determined that the voice had belonged to none other than Galahad the Great. And every goose in every gaggle in all the federation had plainly heard him speak. To Gargle.

Being a goose means that there are certain things that you just know. As any gosling can tell you:

Galahad the Great is the ancient warrior Goose King.

His story has been handed down from the misty dawn of goose lore–grandparent to grandchild, mother goose to newborn hatchling. Every gosling has grown up hearing of his fearsome feats of heroic heraldry.

"*Enemy of the despot,*" *say some.*

"*Defender of the weak,*" *say others.*

"*Galahad aids those whose need is great, but whose bravery and selflessness is greater,*" *say all.*

It has been more than 1,000 years since his voice has last been heard.

"It couldn't be!" shouted the doubters. "It was!" shouted the believers, who were right.

"And what does it mean that we heard it?" everyone wanted to know.

"The decree is simple and clear," the wizened and weathered goose historian patiently wheezed. "Gargle will be our new king." This proclamation was met with great gasps of glee and concerned cries of consternation.

"It can't be!" shouted the doubters. "It is!" shouted the believers, who were right. But all that was settled history now.

There was a funeral to attend.

The mourners were lined in precise rows as far as the eye could see. Like orderly headstones in a military graveyard, the geeses had arranged themselves into the form of a vast, wedge-shaped V. Each goose bowed his or her head in silent respect as the funeral procession crept slowly by. The ornamental catafalque that bore Gargle's body was strapped to Luckless's back with gleaming gold brocade and polished brass buckles. Fat tears streamed down Luckless's recently scrubbed face as he bravely conveyed Gargle's body to the somber white platform located at the uppermost point of the wedge.

Gargle's mother had arranged his wings into two graceful fans over his chest.

She squalled with big trumpeting honks as her son's body solemnly passed the end of her row. His father, overcome with silent grief, stared blankly at the single cloud suspended high in the morning sky. Each member of the Gosworth family leaned gravely forward to place red Chrysanthemums–for devotion and loyalty–around Gargle's head. Curiously, a smile as wide as a summer sky was spread across his face.

On the raised dais stood Gilgamesh the historian, flanked by Loveless to his left. Luckless carefully climbed the stairs and took his place on the right, Gargle's body resting lightly in the pall-draped wooden box on Luckless's strong back. On a small table in front of them burned a large tallow candle set in an ancient bronze candlestick engraved with faded images of Galahad's legendary exploits. Next to the candle sat a large, leatherbound book that looked even older than the candlestick. It was bathed in the light of a dancing taper.

The catafalque containing Gargle was carefully unstrapped by assistants and slowly placed onto the platform at Gilgamesh's webbed feet. Luckless moved to stand above Gargle's head. Loveless moved to his feet. When they had taken their ceremonial places around the body, Gilgamesh began speaking in a low, croaky voice like the spit valve on a trombone.

"Dream time," he began hesitantly. His speech was slow and pregnant with purpose. "A time when geese and men and every creature that walked or crawled or swam or flew beneath the sun and clouds and stars and moon, spoke the same tongue. When mighty giants and wily tricksters strode the earth. When gods and geese were indistinguishable from one another." His gaze swept meaningfully over the federation of mourners. "But that time is gone," his words echoed. "Or is it?"

He extended the tip of his wing to find the correct line on the page of the ancient book laid open before him, adjusted his oval spectacles with his other wing, then continued. "We have gathered here today to honor the memory of our fallen comrade, a beneficent brother, a steadfast son, a firm friend."

A great, cartoonish sob burst from Luckless.

"We mourn the passage of Gargle Gosworth," continued Gilgamesh, "a fine lad who put his friends, his family, and his community before himself." In the second row, Gabbie, Gertie, and Delbert were holding wingtips and snuffling back their tears. "But that young goose is no more."

The historian beheld the gathered multitude. "And in the place of Gargle the Gosling, I give you Gargle the Gander, Grand Guide and Goose King of the Ancient Order of Warriors and Goose Lords, descended from Galahad the Great–a venerated title not bestowed in over a millennium."

Gilgamesh raised his wings above his head and brought them down in a sweeping motion to Gargle's forehead where he sketched the shape of a V with a trace of royal oil. He then placed a goosy crown on the summit of Gargle's resting head.

"Arise Gargle King, and be acknowledged by your loyal subjects!" he bellowed. For a moment, several heartbeats, Gilgamesh's words thundered around them. Then a profound silence washed over the assembled crowd.

In the willow, one of the mockingbirds began to sing her springtime song. Another voice joined the first. Soon, a chorus of mockingbirds was singing a symphony of greeting, heralding a day of harmony, embracing the balance of light and dark, welcoming the advent of the vernal equinox.

It was at this moment of peaceful confluence with creation that a collective gasp erupted from the geesy gathering. All heads turned as one to regard the platform. Dozens of geeses fainted where they stood. Others furiously rubbed their eye sockets with the tips of their flight feathers, unable to believe what their eyeballs were telling them.

Could it be?

Shock was quickly giving way to joy and euphoria.

How could it be?

For there, in front of the assembled throng–on a day that would be sung about for untold generations–history jumped from the dry and dreary pages of time into the stout and beating heart of the world.

Gargle was sitting up!

And smiling!

Astonishment. Simple, electric *astonishment* pulsed though the throbbing veins of every goose. No one spoke. No one dared to even breathe. Even the mockingbirds stopped singing, rendered voiceless by the dumbfounding scene.

Milking it for all it was worth, Gargle rose dramatically to his little feet and hopped somewhat gracelessly onto the platform, being careful to conceal his amusement at the kerfuffle. "I am your king," he stuttered, his voice cracking with an adolescent twang.

He looked down at the first row where his mother had collapsed into the rolls of fat on Delbert's ample belly. Delbert, meanwhile, was furiously fanning Mrs. Gosworth's floppy face with his tweed hat. "And here is my first royal act," Gargle loudly proclaimed, finding his kingly voice.

He cast a look at Gilgamesh who produced a gleaming silver scepter nearly as tall as Gargle. Its staff had been fashioned to resemble a column of twisting smoke crowned with a golden goose, its wings outspread to their maximum span, its feet rooted firmly atop a shimmering golden egg. Gargle pointed it at Luckless then waved it theatrically, almost dropping it in the process. His face broke into a wide grin.

"My loyal friend and most trusted confidant," he began. "From this day forth, you will be an esteemed member of our goosing federation, accorded all the benefits and entitlements of full enrollment in our society." Luckless's Adam's apple bobbed up and down in his throat like a lobbed tennis ball as he gulped back his confusion.

"And as such," continued Gargle, "you will no longer be referred to as *Luckless* the Donkey, henceforth, your name is to be Sir *Lucky* the Donkey, and you will be treated with the love and the respect that you so richly deserve."

"Sir Lucky!" the crowd roared in unison.

Gargle touched each of Sir Lucky's shoulders with his scepter, indicating that his word was now law. Gargle turned to face Loveless. Her eyes were deep, round pools in which Gargle could see himself. "And you," he said, tenderly lifting her chin with his wing, his little goosy heart brimming with limitless affection. "What is your wish, my brave, sweet jenny? Name it, and it is yours."

She locked eyes with Sir Lucky. "I want him," she simply said, indicating Sir Lucky with her hoof.

"And so it shall be!" shouted Gargle the King. "From this day to your last, the two of you are betrothed as equals, as life mates, as husband and wife." He touched the tip of his scepter to her heart and then did the same to Sir Lucky. Gargle spun to face the federation of witnesses and proclaimed, "I give you your first royal couple, the Duke and Duchess of Donkeydom, the right and Honorable Sir Lucky and Lady Lovey! Love and honor them!" It was a law happily obeyed by all.

With the ceremony completed, the majority of the Federation left to begin the complex preparations for the Great Departure to the northern goosing grounds. As king, Gargle would act as grand guide in the first gaggle at the vanguard of the migration.

His friends and family gathered with him beneath the whispering canopy of the willow tree. "But how did you survive?" Sir Lucky hee-hawed in bewilderment.

Gargle considered the question for a moment, his brow knitting into a V of perplexity. "I'm not sure," was all he could say with any certainty. "The last thing I remember is you and Lady Lovey ramming me through the barn wall, followed by the thunderclap of an enormous bell. I saw an imposing goosy form showered in brilliant white light. Whoever it was spoke to me. He said, 'Well done, my brave, bold lad.' That was it."

Everyone was peering at him with bottomless respect, their faces agog with amazement. A mockingbird trilled a run of three melodious notes. The sun peeked through the branches. Gargle's little heart thumped heavily in his chest.

"When I woke up, I was being cared for by Gilgamesh and his assistants. I pleaded with them to let me see my friends and family, but they explained that no one could see me for three days. That was the law." A tone of exasperation ran through the group.

"They also told me that I was being prepared for my coronation and that tradition decrees there be a funeral for the old self. That Gargle the Gosling was dead and gone. I was to be reborn as Gargle the King!"

He looked at Sir Lucky, a hint of his old self shining through. "And boy did I live it up! An endless buffet of hot dogs and old candy and stale bread and spilled soda–everything I love!"

His mother made a pinchy face. "So for three days you listened to us weep and wail and you didn't do a thing to let us know?"

"What could I do?" said Gargle defensively. "This is the way that Galahad wanted it," he added with a tinge of reverence in his voice.

"Oh, what's the difference?" his father interrupted, shouldering his way to his

boy's side. "We have him back and that's all that really matters! All hail Gargle the King," he loudly honked.

They shuffled into a ring around him and each bent a knee to their newly crowned king. "Hail!" they proclaimed together, standing wingtip-to-wingtip. The warmth of the spring day had fully blossomed.

Gargle the King looked at his friend, Sir Lucky, and winked.

Just inside the edge of the trees encircling the old mill pond, a dark crimson figure slinked unnoticed along the ground.

A pair of almond-shaped eyes burned with an ignominious flame as they scowled toward the willow tree.

The lone creature slowly withdrew into a briar patch and vanished.

And the old, wily world turned like a wheel.

And geeses lived and gooses loved.

And the crickets sang and sang and sang.

The End

Goosolalia
Important Concepts in Goosespeak

Barrel roll. An aerial maneuver in which an aircraft, or in this case a goose, turns in a corkscrew pattern in midair. This trick is highly discouraged in flight school because it is unsafe around other fliers.

Call sign. The term referring to the aviation nicknames given to high-ranking *geeses* in a given *gaggle*. (See "Mother Goose")

"Canada Goose" versus "Canadian Goose." This is an old, old argument in the goose community that has never been resolved, mostly because geeses love arguing too much to ever reach a final answer. For those sick of hearing about it, "goose" works just fine.

Ear-hole. The listening vents in the sides of a goose's head. Because *geeses* so often disagree with one another, the act of actually listening to someone carries a lot of emotional baggage. "Get the feathers out of your ear-holes" is a common expression in *Goosespeak*.

Federation of gaggles. The Goosespeak term for the hundreds, oftentimes thousands of individual gaggles participating in a *Great Departure* ritual. It is also a term that expresses a show of goosish force through strength in numbers.

Flight School. The mandatory training that every young gosling must attend in order to perfect her or his flying techniques. Flight school classes include "Using Your *Internal Compass*," "Storm Clouds: Friend or Foe?," "Commercial Airliners & You," "The Perfect Two-Point Landing," "Ground and Water Landings," and nearly everyone's favorite "Emergency Aerial Maneuvers." Importantly, flight school is required to qualify for a higher individual gaggle ranking in the *Great Departure*.

First Gaggle. The *skein* at the *vanguard* of the *Great Departure*. It is a tremendous honor for the *gaggle* that is chosen.

Flyway. The open path in a *staging area* where gaggles achieve liftoff. Many collisions occur here. Goslings are taught never to play in or near the flyway! In Goosespeak, "You can't get out of the flyway" is a saying that means you don't understand something important, or you are simply clumsy.

Foie gras. A controversial French delicacy made up of fatty goose or duck liver. Understandably, ducks and geeses are opposed to it.

The letter "g." This is the most significant letter in the goose alphabet. Every individual in a given *gaggle* has a first and last name that begins with this letter. The letter "g" also contains historical significance, tracing its roots back to the ancient warrior Goose King, **Galahad the Great.**

Gaggle. Technically, a flock of *geeses* that isn't in flight. A gaggle is equal to at least five geeses. While the term originally meant an unorganized group of geeses standing around with nothing to do, it has evolved over the centuries to mean an extended goose family unit. (Often interchangeable with the term "skein.")

Galahad the Great. The ancient warrior Goose King, Galahad the Great is an important figure from goose mythology. In addition to being the reason why every goose name (first and last) begins with the letter "g," he is also said to aid heroic geeses in times of epic need. Hearing his voice is proof that you have been anointed by his gallantry, graciousness, generosity, gentility, and general goodness.

Giant dumps. Geeses are embarrassed to admit it, but they expel rather large "butt nuggets" everywhere they go. Lower-ranking teenage ganders have been known to have contests to see whose is the most impressive. Goose parents, *mother gooses* in particular, consider this a poor topic of conversation.

"Gooses" vs. "geeses." Never mind. This one will never be solved.

Goosespeak. The time-honored linguistic tongue of the ancient Goose Lords. To human ears, it sounds like someone stepping on a duck. (See "goosolalia")

Goosing Grounds. The ancient destination point, or terminus, after the three traditional *rest stop ponds* on the Great Departure's flight route. Over the years, many of the geeses's once great ponds and lakes have been taken over by humans and turned into parking lots, freeway overpasses, and in one famous case, a Peking duck restaurant. (See "Great Goosing Grounds")

Goosolalia. The term for individual words and phrases in *Goosespeak*. To animals (including humans) not fluent in this language, it sounds like nonsensical, farty gibberish.

Gosling. A baby goose. Also, a common putdown in the cafeteria pond at flight school. Often associated with anything yellow.

Grand Guide. The very highest honor in a *federation of gaggles.* This is conferred on a goose who has accomplished mighty deeds of goosing greatness. Not only does the Grand Guide take the first rotation of *point* in his or her own family gaggle, but is also given Point in the *first gaggle* at the *vanguard* of the Great Departure. Essentially, the Grand Guide is the leader of the entire goose population in a given migration. Any goose anointed king holds this exalted title for life. All fledgling fliers dream of earning this important designation.

Great Departure. The ancient goose ritual of migrating south in the autumn and north in the spring.

Great Goosing Grounds. The goosespeak term for goose heaven in the afterlife. Referred to as "the 3 Gs" in goosespeak slang.

Guide. The leader at any given time at the *point* of the V in an individual gaggle.

Hard Deck. In goose aviation, the maximum altitude for flight. Fledglings are taught never to fly above the *hard deck* because of the thin air (causes loss of lift) and the lack of oxygen (causes loss of life).

Headwind. A wind that blows directly into your face, necessary for achieving liftoff. In one of their first lessons in *flight school*, fledglings are asked to achieve liftoff in a tailwind. It does not work and is often comical, leading to friendly teasing.

Honking. Many people wonder why geeses are so noisy when they're in flight. According to Gargle, when they are in formation, the goose in point position needs constant updates on weather, wind speed, airborne obstacles like birds and planes, cloud formations, and other aviation and meteorological data. Gaggle members not on point provide the leader with all of this as well as shouts of encouragement. They are also honking out their call signs to keep the radio channels clear and the formation tight. It shouldn't be overlooked that geeses truly love to fly, so some of them are simply honking out their joy at how beautiful it is to be a goose soaring through a gloriously blue sky!

Internal compass. Every gosling is born with one. It is a little-known fact that a goose has the best sense of direction in the world. It is very difficult for a goose to get lost, though it has been known to happen.

Migration Route. The ancient flight path taken to both the northern and southern *goosing grounds*. It is the same in either direction, using the same *rest stop ponds* along the way. The path was determined by Galahad the Great. As such, the migration route has never changed.

Mother Goose. This Goosespeak term has many meanings. 1) It is the radio *call sign* for the goose in *point* position in any given *gaggle*, regardless of gender; 2) It is an honored social title in goose culture given to an elderly female goose who is a gifted storyteller and extraordinary gossip; 3) It is a high compliment; 4) It is the elemental maternal figure from which all geeses descend; 5) It is the quintessence, the crux, the heart, the core, the lifeblood, the spirit, the soul of goosiness; 6) It is all of the above and so very much more.

Point. The lead position in the flying wedge, or *skein*. (See "guide")

Point Guide. The honorific title/position given to the highest ranking members of a gaggle. This designation grants them the right to take *point* in a *great departure.* (See "grand guide")

Rest stop ponds. The waypoints along the ancient *migration route* where a goose can stop for a bite to eat, get some sleep, and perhaps take a *giant dump.* There are three of them along the way.

Skein. A single gaggle of geeses in flight. (Often interchangeable with "gaggle.")

Staging area. The location at a great departure where geeses are assembled into their proper gaggles for takeoff.

The letter "V." The original significance of this letter is highly disputed. Some geeses argue that gaggles take this formation because it represents the importance of the honored *vanguard* position. Other geeses maintain that it comes from the Roman numeral five (V), the minimum number of geeses needed to make up a gaggle. No one knows for sure which story is right and no one probably ever will.

Vanguard. The point of the V in the *first gaggle* of a *great departure.*

Yellow. The color of *goslings.* Often mistaken by the non-goose world to mean "cowardly." In Goosespeak, it is simply a mild putdown meaning that someone is "acting like a baby."

Andrew Perry, Author

Andrew Perry spent the first eighteen years of his life growing up in the small town of Spencerport, New York, along the banks of the Erie Canal. By all accounts, his childhood had a normal amount of exciting episodes and troubling incidents. He was once attacked by a goose while kayaking.

At college in Oswego, Brockport and Cincinnati, his love of reading and writing led him to the decision that this might be a decent way to make a living. He was right. He teaches First Year Composition in the University Writing Program at the Rochester Institute of Technology, along the banks of the Genesee River. He lives with his beloved wife Kimberly and their inexcusably adorable dog, Tipsy, in a house that was built a long time ago where they eat and drink and enjoy life considerably.

Gargle the Goose is Andrew's first book. His fondest wish is that you fall as deeply in love with Gargle as he has.

Elaine Verstraete, Illustrator

Artist Elaine Verstraete, an illustrator, teacher and musician, creates from her hilltop studio in Middlesex, NY. A graduate of Syracuse University with a BFA from the school of Visual and Performing Arts, Elaine has been a freelance illustrator since 1987. Her images have appeared nationally on Christmas and Easter seals for the American Lung Association, on numerous Rochester, NY event posters - including the 2014 Lilac Festival, and on packaging labels for Wegmans Markets. Elaine garnered early inspiration from painters Norman Rockwell, Andrew Wyeth and N.C Wyeth. Her figurative watercolors first attracted Children's Book Publishers for whom she illustrated numerous historical biographies and the award-winning picture book The Star of Christmas (Winterlake Press). Elaine has worked as an Adjunct Professor at RIT since 2002. She currently teaches Illustration at Finger Lakes Community College. She lives with her life partner, David, along with their three cats, Shogun, Django and Fila.

Made in the USA
Middletown, DE
05 November 2019